EXETER EXCAVATIONS: THE GUILDHALL SITE

by

John Collis MA

Preface

LAST year, on the eve of the excavations described in this pamphlet, the University published a booklet by Lady Fox, *Exeter in Roman times*, in which she summarized what we then knew about *Isca Dumnoniorum*, knowledge derived largely from her own excavations in war-damaged Exeter in 1945–47 and later. The new programme is now under way. Mr John Collis, at the time a member of the History Department, University of Exeter, has completed a season's excavations on the 'Guildhall site', and gives us here his first report. He has stripped the layers of deposits from a relatively large area and has paid equal attention to all levels. Readers of this pamphlet will see how much of the past a trained archaeologist can reconstruct from evidence which the ordinary observer would ignore or fail to understand. If we want to know more about the remote history of our ancient city we must set archaeologists to work whenever the opportunity occurs.

FRANK BARLOW

May 1972   *Professor of History, University of Exeter*

EXETER EXCAVATIONS:
THE GUILDHALL SITE

THE large area behind the Guildhall between North Street and Goldsmith Street which is scheduled for development in the next year or two (Fig. 1) is now an open space given over to temporary car parks. Only a handful of small buildings stand, isolated and stranded, to recall the maze of densely-packed lanes, back-alleys and courtyards, filled with the warehouses, shops and small businesses, which were demolished in recent years. This complex was largely the product of the expansion of the town in the nineteenth century, but here and there buildings such as St Pancras Church or the merchants' houses in North Street have survived to recall an earlier period. But the strongest mark of the middle ages lay in the system of streets and property boundaries which defined and restricted all later developments. The layout of this system dates from a period for which documentary evidence tells us little or nothing about the character and economic development of the town, and for this only archaeological and topographical studies can advance our knowledge. Indeed archaeology can throw considerable light on periods as late as the eighteenth century, in providing tangible evidence of the trades and industries of Exeter which the documents cannot give us.

But underneath this present town, whose origin rests essentially in late Saxon and early Medieval times, lies an earlier town, of which nothing remains visible except the circuit of the defensive walls. The Roman town of *Isca Dumnoniorum* was the regional capital, the major town of the South West, and the evidence for it has recently been reviewed by Lady Fox in her pamphlet, *Exeter in Roman Times*. The redevelopment area falls within the circuit of the Roman defences, and is thus likely to produce remains of that period. Indeed finds of mosaic pavements were made in Waterbeer Street during the eighteenth and nineteenth centuries, indicating the presence of luxurious private houses.

Thus the ten acres to be redeveloped offer us an opportunity to discover more about the development of Exeter. Did it have its origin as a major fort, during Vespasian's conquest of southern England? What was the nature of the civil settlement which developed later into the Roman town? Did anything of Roman life survive into the Saxon period? Is there evidence of late Saxon occupation, and when were the

3

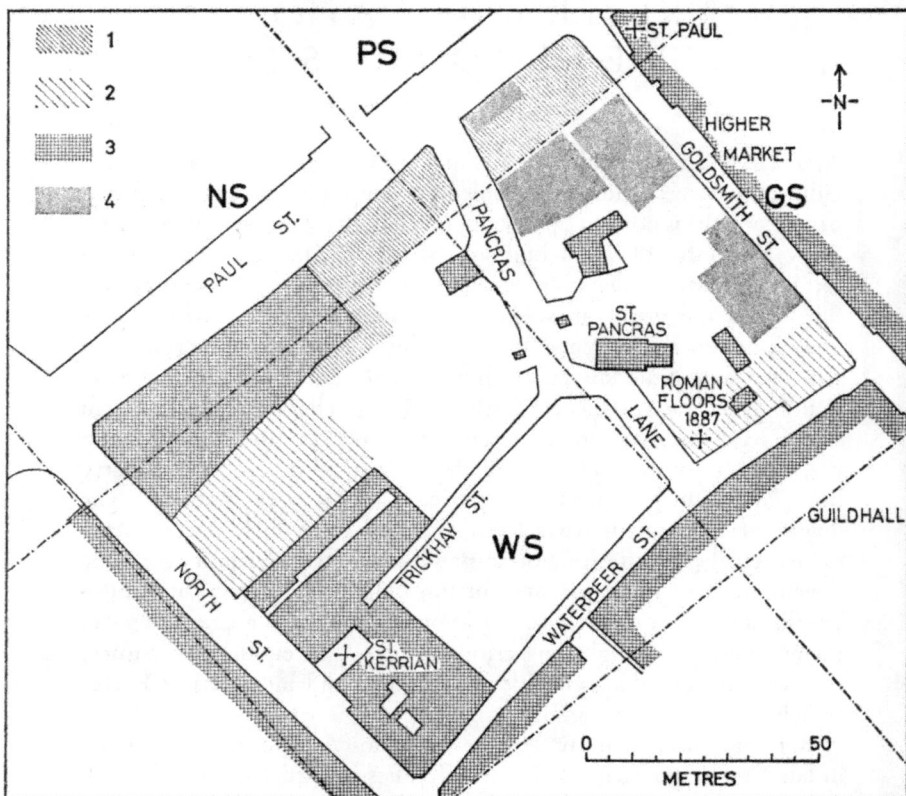

Fig. 1   The 'Guildhall' site, showing the excavation grid.

(1) Areas totally disturbed by terracing.
(2) Areas partly disturbed.
(3) Buildings still standing, summer 1971.
(4) Excavated areas in Goldsmith Street (GS).

present streets and boundaries laid out? These were some of the questions with which we started. Some we have partly answered; others will need further research.

But the redevelopment does not merely give us opportunities; it also imposes a burden on us, for the construction of the new buildings will result in extensive damage to, if not complete destruction for all time of, the archaeological deposits. When we started we had restrictions of both time and money for our work, though our original dead-line has receded and a second season of excavation is now possible. The area is much too large for complete excavation, and we have concentrated on those areas which will be most completely destroyed in the redevelopment. These consist mainly of the present street frontages, but even here work is yet further restricted by previous terracing of the hillside along Paul Street, or the construction of cellars, both of which have already destroyed anything of interest. In 1971 the frontages in Pancras Lane and Goldsmith Street received attention; in 1972 it will be the turn of Waterbeer Street and North Street.

The results and finds from Goldsmith Street are now being prepared for publication, but as the report will take some time to prepare, and be of specialist interest, we hope this pamphlet will fill the gap by offering more immediate publication of some of the major results, and of the more interesting of the rich and varied finds. The discoveries will be described period by period, starting with the earliest. The accompanying plans are based on our artificial grid of 100 metre squares, and grid references, like GS 29-86, can be given to any metre square in the grid. The first number is a reading from left to right on the plans, the second from bottom to top, in the same way as on Ordnance Survey maps.

The first century A.D. (Fig. 2)
Other than a few scraps of worked flint, there is no evidence of occupation before the Roman conquest. But dating from the first two or three decades after the conquest (about 50–80 A.D.) are a series of massive timber buildings, laid out at a slight angle to Goldsmith Street, on the orientation which was to be followed by all the later Roman structures. There were at least three main phases of construction. The two earlier stages ran on approximately the same lines as the third phase, and only survived where the walls diverged slightly, especially around GS 40-40. The final phase consisted of two large buildings some 40 metres long, standing back to back, and a third at right angles at the south end. All that survives are slots cut into the natural clay, into which timbers, probably horizontal sill beams, had been inserted. Only in one case did actual traces of the timbers survive, the outline of three upright rectangular posts in GS 23-85. Otherwise the timber had been systematically dug out when the buildings were demolished, and the resulting slots filled with clay. It is the pottery, and one or two coins from these slots, which will eventually allow us to assign a date for their demolition.

What these buildings are is as yet far from clear. They are not the normal barrack blocks one would expect inside a military fort, though

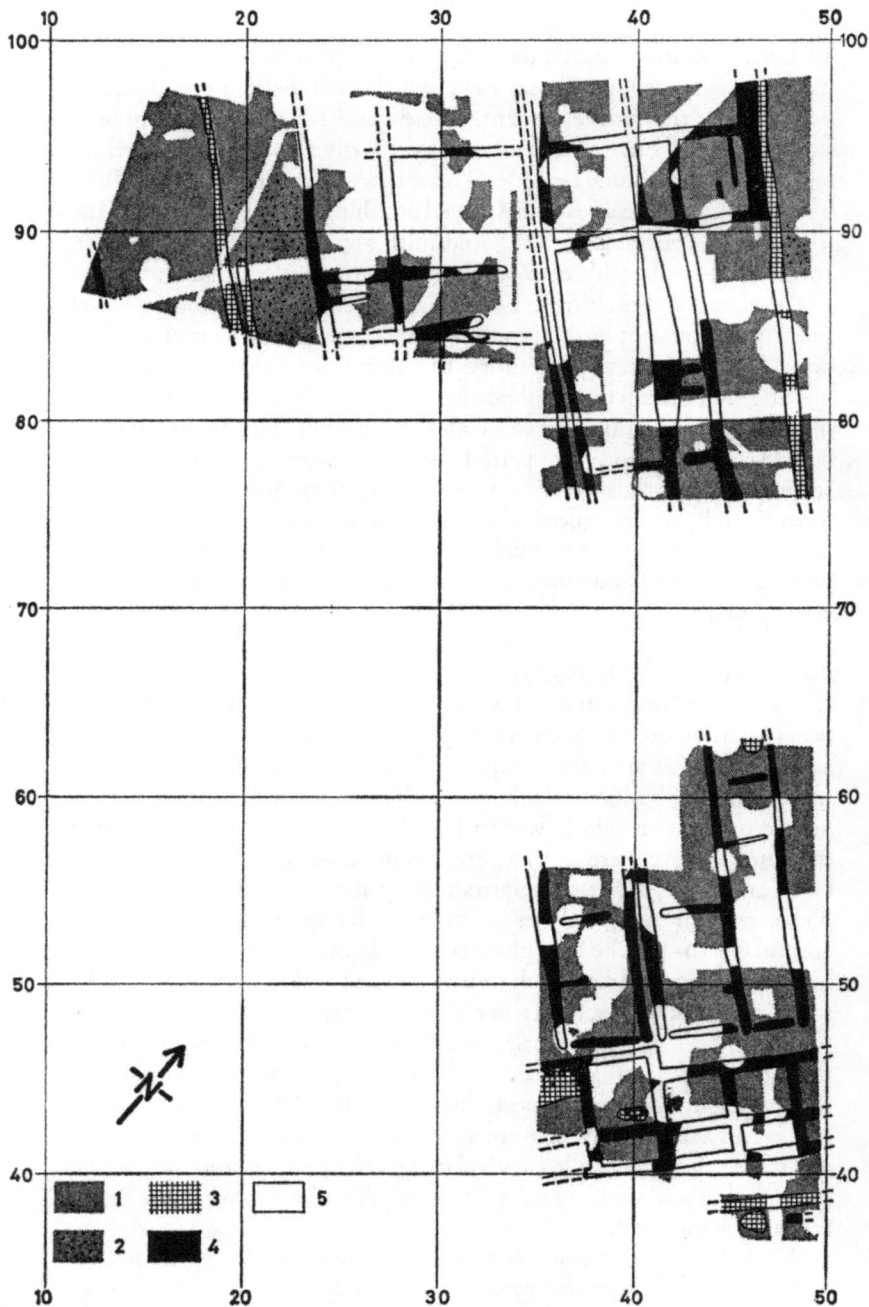

Fig. 2 Plan of the latest phase of early Roman timber buildings (late first century A.D.).
(1) Undisturbed deposits.   (2) Cobbled areas.   (3) Pits and open drains.
(4) Wall slots.   (5) Later disturbances, or unexcavated.   Each square is 10m x 10m.

at this early period Roman military architecture had not become as stereotyped as it was later. Traces of military defences of a fort have already been discovered on the site of the South Gate, but the new discoveries imply a more extensive establishment. The massive scale and lay-out speaks against a civil origin, as does the systematic demolition. A provisional interpretation would see these as timber buildings in a large fort, at whose centre stands the stone building (possibly a bath building) found in 1971 beneath St Mary Major.

The two North-South buildings of the later phase consist of three or four parallel slots. In the eastern building there are slots at right angles defining small rooms, and at the northern end the building widens out to the east (GS 47–92). In plan this resembles the classic barrack block for housing a 'century', the men being quartered in the long narrow part of the building, the officers in the wide end. To the east runs an open drain, a necessity on the heavy clay soil, and beyond it traces of cobbling suggest a pathway dividing this from further blocks. The patchy western building is more ambiguous, but to the west it too had a small cobbled pathway with a drain, and to the west of that another timber building. Hardly any trace of the floor levels survived, but in GS 37–50 was found the remains of a clay oven. The East–West building at the southern end also resembles a barrack block in its final stage, but it is rather narrower than the other two buildings.

The second century
After the demolition of the building a clayey brown soil formed over the site, perhaps the product of cultivation. The whole of the area in the northern part of our excavation was to remain an open space until the fourth century, except for an open gully dug for some reason diagonally N–S across the site, a rough stone wall, presumably a boundary wall, and a few pits apparently dug for clay. It appears that the houses of Roman Exeter covered only a part of the area enclosed by the walls.

Further south, nearer the town centre, the development was different. Perhaps before the end of the first century there was some industrial activity in the form of large hearths made of burnt clay. Their purpose is unclear, but the largest have a diameter of three to four metres. To the north was a rubbish dump, with masses of oyster shells. Then sometime in the first quarter of the second century development of the area took place with the construction of two new timber buildings. The boundary between these buildings follows the approximate line GS 42–40/40–56 and this line was to be respected by all subsequent buildings, with different developments to east or west of the line.

The best preserved of all the timber buildings was the first that was constructed west of the boundary line. Parts of four rooms have been excavated. Two had simple earthen floors but the other two were of *opus signinum,* Roman concrete made of lime and crushed brick, set on a pitched stone foundation. At the junction of wall and floor was a quarter-round moulding (Plate 2). The walls consisted of sleeper beams laid in slight slots in the soil; within the timber frame was placed wattle and daub, and the inside walls were then plastered and painted. In one room was found a pile of small black and white *tesserae,* which had never been used, suggesting that there had been plans to construct a mosaic floor. This building only lasted a generation or so and was replaced by a series of simple shacks with earthen or mortar floors, which date towards the end of the second century. On the eastern part of the site only one phase of timber building was encountered.

The third century (Fig. 3)
It is difficult to date the beginning of the next phase. The main problem is that all the floor levels of the late Roman and medieval phases have been terraced away in post-medieval times, and all we find are features such as pits and wall-footings cut into the underlying deposits. However, at some time in the late-second or early-third centuries the timber buildings were swept away to make room for two massive stone-built houses.

The western building only ran a little into our excavation at GS 35–42, but a corner of a wall in GS 31–82 is apparently the northern limit of the same building. It had tesselated and mosaic pavements and a slate roof to judge by the surrounding debris. To the east we have part of a house-type familiar from other Roman towns, with a corridor flanking a series of rooms which partly underlies Goldsmith Street. Two of these rooms had hypocaust heating systems, and one of these a tesselated pavement, fragments of which had collapsed into the channels below. The walls of the buildings were made mainly of pitched trap footings with coursed blocks set in mortar in the upper levels. There was also evidence of substantial alterations and additions to the house during its century or so of habitation.

The fourth century (Fig. 3)
Around the western house are two gullies; one (GS 18–84) runs east–west, the other (GS 37–42) north–south. Their relationship to the

Plate 1   Marble head of an unknown man. Late-first century A.D. Height 72mm.

Plate 2   Timber building looking North, with *opus signinum* floors in the foreground and behind the ranging pole. Early-second century A.D.

Plate 3 Late-medieval pit lined with a wooden barrel.

Plate 4 Late-medieval parish and property boundary walls, with late-Roman gullies in the background. Pancras Lane area, looking North West.

Plate 5   Stone-lined pit with peat filling at GS 43–38, looking South. Sixteenth century.

Plate 6   Cultivation trenches and parish boundary wall, looking East from Pancras Lane. Late-sixteenth century.

Plate 7a   Decorated leather knife scabbard. Length 150mm.

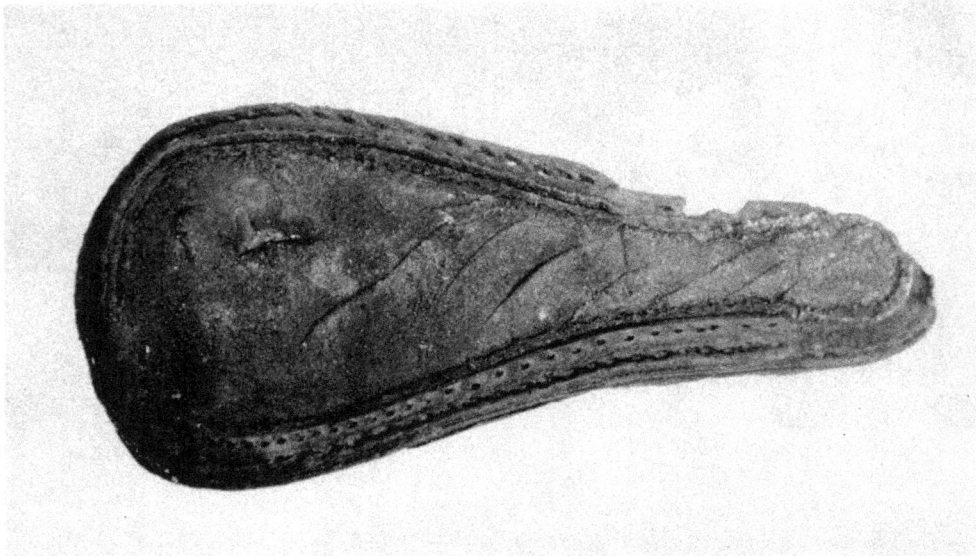

Plate 7b   Leather sole of a shoe, length 213mm. Both scabbard and sole come from the pit at GS 43–38. Sixteenth century.

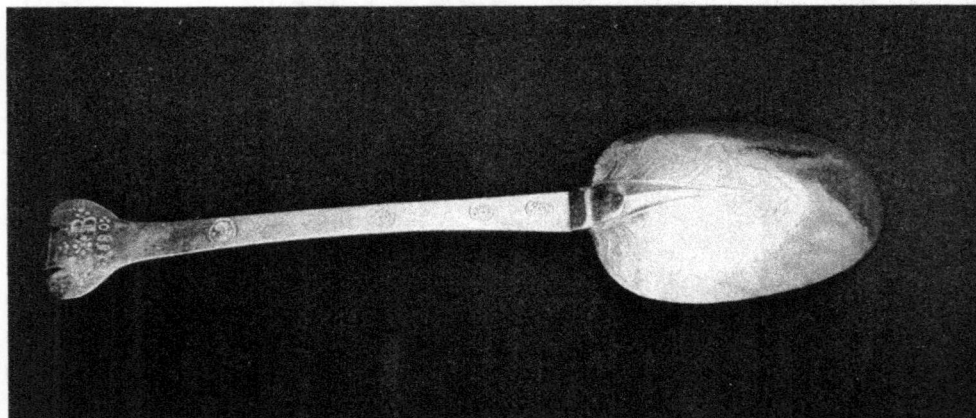

Plate 8   Decorated silver spoon. Late-seventeenth century Exeter hallmarks, with inscription dated 1680. From a latrine pit. Length 191mm.

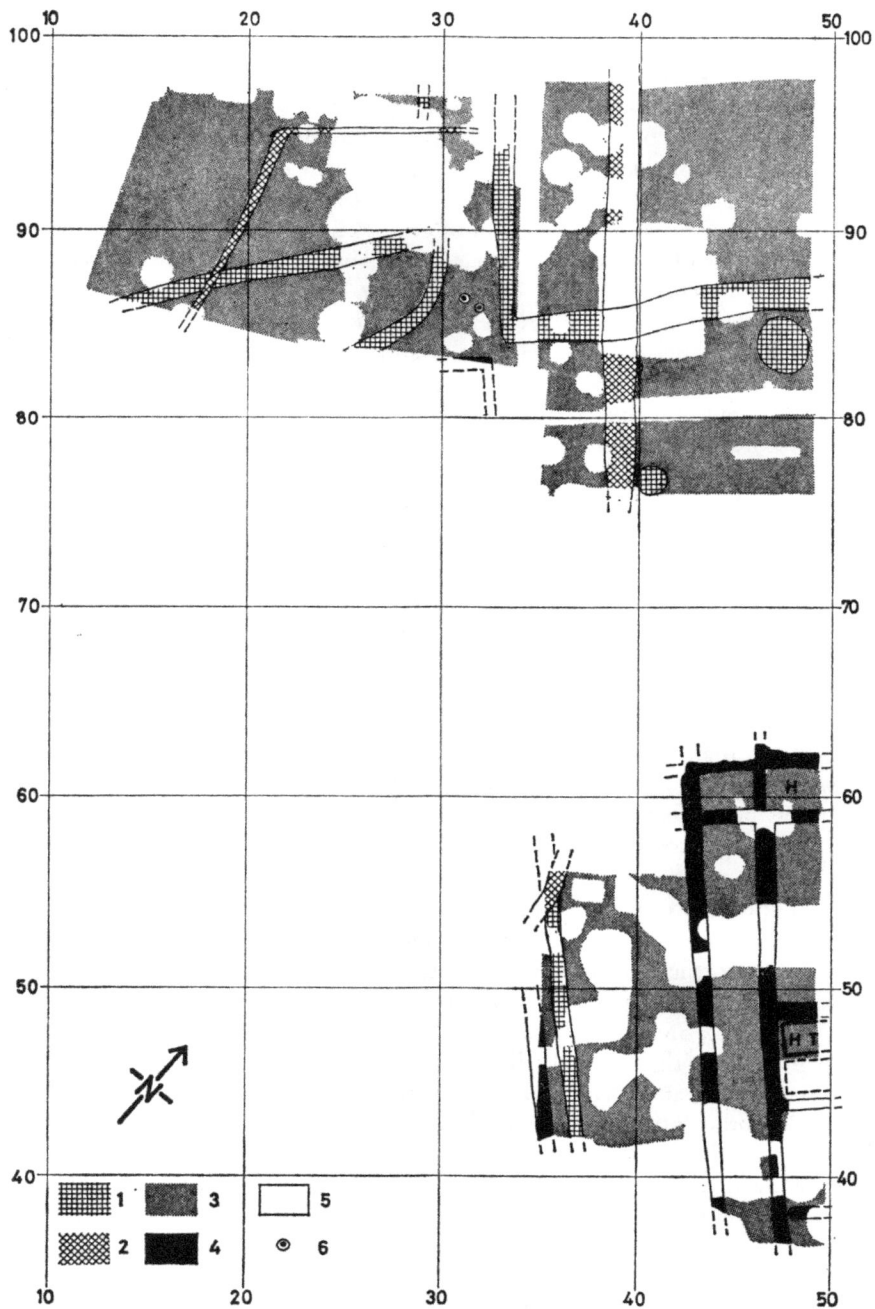

Fig. 3 Plan of late Roman phase (third-fourth centuries A.D.).   (1) Pits or ditches,
late third-early fourth centuries.   (2) Ditches, fourth century or later.
(3) Undisturbed deposits.   (4) Stone walls.   (5) Unexcavated or disturbed areas.
(6) Postholes.

building—contemporary or later—is obscure but both were partly filled with rubble derived from the destruction of the house, along with pottery of fourth century date. Thus the houses were perhaps in a state of dilapidation by the early-fourth century. These gullies seem to be contemporary with a ditched enclosure in the north–east corner of our area. In the infill of one of its ditches at GS 47–86 were the skulls of a number of horses and cows, as though animals were being butchered nearby. At a yet later date, similar though more irregular boundary gullies were cut across the area. Dating evidence is meagre, but they pre-date the twelfth century, and cut through the early-fourth-century gullies and the Roman buildings. From one of these gullies came a marble head of an unknown man (Plate 1). According to Professor Jocelyn Toynbee the head is carved in a Mediterranean style and dates from the late first century A.D., and so was old when buried. It was possibly a memorial bust such as was often set up at tombs or in private houses.

Early Medieval (Eleventh to thirteenth centuries)
It appears that by the eleventh century the area was deserted. At present our knowledge of the chronological development of medieval pottery in Exeter is almost negligible, and the finds from the 1971 excavations represent a major step forward, though work has yet to start on an analysis of the pottery. Most of the medieval finds come from pits. Some of these, from their distinctive green infill, are clearly cess pits; others are wells or simple rubbish pits. Most of the pottery is of local coarse ware, mainly cooking pots, but there are also finer wares, much of which was imported from France. From the twelfth century there are white vessels with splashes of red paint, and storage jars with applied strips, finger-printed like pastry crust, both types from northern France. Later there are glazed wares, white or buff fabrics, including sherds with apple green glaze, probably from the Bordeaux area, and sherds with red and orange glazes from Rouen. Eventually the pits will tell us much about the growth and density of settlement at each period. Provisionally, it appears that the earliest, eleventh-century, pits are confined to the southern end of the site, and only in the twelfth century does settlement expand north to Paul Street. Most of the pits occur in back gardens of houses which presumably front on to the streets, but no trace of the houses themselves survive. Occasionally pits occur on the street frontage, implying a gap in the frontage, and also late pits tend to be further back from the frontage, due perhaps to houses expanding back into the garden plots. The clay

subsoil has caused some of the pits to become water-logged, preserving timber and wood, leather and other organic remains. One early pit produced a leather belt. A later one contained a silver penny identified by Mr Dolley as of Henry III, and a second coin of the same king was found in garden soil in Pancras Lane.

The layout of streets and properties must belong to this period (Fig. 1). The street system is based on a fairly regular grid, similar to those found in the fortified 'burhs' laid out in late Saxon times at places like Winchester. It has been claimed that Exeter's system is of this date, but at present we have no evidence for its existence earlier than the twelfth century. Some of the medieval churches such as St Kerrian in North Street and St Paul on the corner of Goldsmith Street and Paul Street were laid out on the street grid and orientated with it, rather than truly East–West. These churches certainly existed by the late-twelfth, and perhaps already in the mid-twelfth century, so the streets also existed by then. A property boundary (GS 15–98/ 23–98) which later became a parish boundary was certainly respected by a series of pits of twelfth-century date. The church of St Pancras in the middle of the area, however, is not related to the streets, but is truly East–West. Pancras Lane merely provides access from Waterbeer Street to its entrance. The implication is that it predates the streets, but unfortunately we know nothing of its origin, only that it existed in the twelfth century.

Late medieval (Thirteenth to fifteenth centuries)
Knowledge of this period is still largely derived from pits. One water-logged well had been lined with a wooden barrel, one of the best examples found in the country (Plate 3), and another produced a tub lid incised with a cross and pentacle. Imported pottery was still predominantly from south–west France, though the standard of local potting was rising considerably. One large rectangular pit in GS 39–36 was lined with wood, and was probably the predecessor of two sixteenth-century stone-lined pits discussed below. Back gardens were now defined by stone walls (Plate 4), built of trap, and one house at least was provided with a stone built drain.

The sixteenth century (Fig. 4 and cover)
This century was one of great prosperity in Exeter, and our finds of this period are especially rich and interesting. Mention has already been made of two stone-lined pits, GS 35–40 and GS 45–38, both of which were water-logged and filled with peat (Plate 5). The original

purpose of the pits is obscure. They certainly had contained water, and leather-tanning seems a possibility. But both were left to fill in slowly, and, amongst the rubbish, finds such as boots and shoes (Plate 7b), wooden bowls, leather scabbards (Plate 7a), utensils of various sorts, fragments of furniture, cloth, and many other items which decay under normal conditions were preserved. Evidence of local trades included shoe making, with leather off-cuts and two possible shoe-lasts, marked with the numbers VIII and VIIII, perhaps indicating sizes, and also metal working, with discarded jets from moulding pewter. There was a pewter bowl with an incised design, and a mass of broken glass. Unfortunately this was badly decayed and crushed, and only a little can be reconstructed, but it may well prove to be some of the earliest products of the local glass industry. There was also an early glass mirror, set in a disc of wood, with a covering of gold sheet. From the bottom of one pit came substantial portions of three south west French ('Saintonge') jugs, two decorated with multicoloured paint in the so-called 'polychrome' style. One has typical motifs of shields flanked by coloured birds outlined in black, and the other has a moulded human mask under the rim. Such vessels are usually dated late-thirteenth/early-fourteenth century, but the Exeter finds must lead to a reconsideration of this dating, including that of the famous Exeter 'puzzle jug' which is in the same fabric. From the top of the pit come fragments of several stoneware jugs, one with its hinged pewter lid still intact. These are products of the Rhenish potteries, and are regular imports until the eighteenth century. The best examples from our pit are decorated with floral designs—acorns, roses, etc.— and should date from the third quarter of the fifteenth century. They were probably made in Cologne.

Further to the north (GS 33–54 and 40–50), a couple of pits produced a mass of broken pottery which clearly includes wasters from a kiln in the vicinity. Some are warped, others had broken in firing, as glaze on the fractures betrays, and others had slates, which had been used as *setters* to separate the pots in the kiln, still adhering to the rims. Fragments of these slate *setters,* covered in glaze, were scattered over a considerable area. The products of the kiln include glazed jugs, bowls, cooking pots and storage jars, often with frilled strips around their necks. Production was probably in the decade or two before 1550.

The property fronting on to Pancras Lane (GS 11–84/23–98) was being used for some horticultural purpose in the sixteenth century. A series of six or seven parallel trenches, up to a metre across and half a metre deep were dug across the site from east to west (Plate 6). They

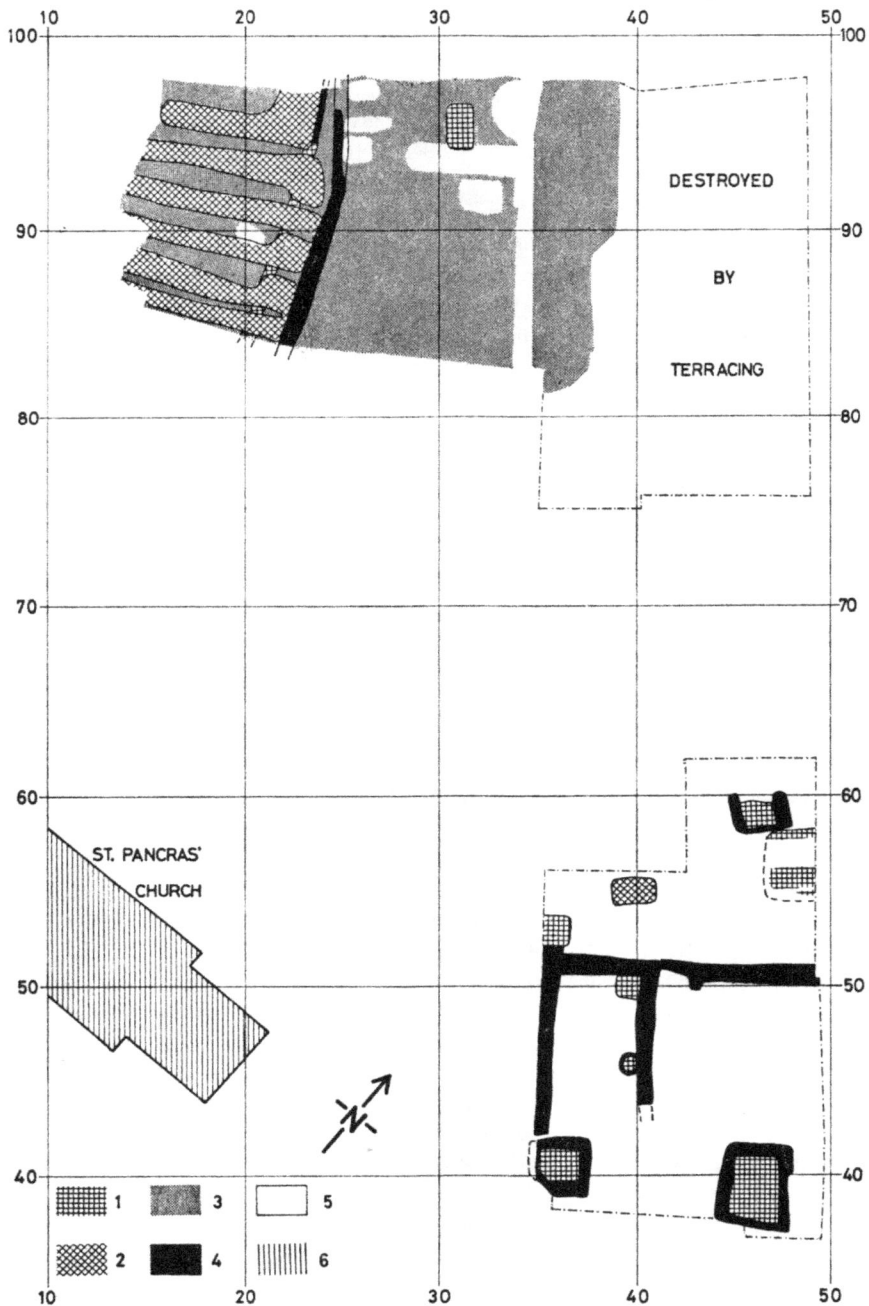

Fig. 4 Plan of sixteenth-century features. (1) Early sixteenth century. (2) Late-sixteenth-century ditches or pits. (3) Undisturbed garden deposits. (4) Stone walls. (5) Later disturbances or unexcavated. (6) Surviving building.

were then filled with a mixture of clay, plaster and rubble. Professor Maurice Barley has suggested they may have been for viticulture, and there is certainly documentary evidence for vines in Exeter at this period. Grape pips were among the organic remains from the pits. Dating evidence for the trenches comes from the pottery, including stoneware decorated with figures, local pottery, bronze jettons (token coinage), a silver coin, and an encaustic tile, perhaps Flemish, dated 1556.

Late in the century we have the first map of Exeter by Hogenberg, drawn in 1587. The Goldsmith Street frontage (cover) is shown fully built up, but this can only have been the case for a short time previously, for there was at least one open space as late as 1550. Of the sixteenth century houses little trace remains, victims again of later terracing. Only one or two walls were given deeper foundations, showing a construction of irregular lumps of trap set in brown clay. A new refinement was the appearance of indoor latrine pits—warmer though more smelly than the external! Also depicted on the Hogenberg map is a wall joining properties in Paul Street with St Pancras Church. This wall, a rebuilding of a fifteenth-century wall, was found in the excavation, and with some patching it remained in use for another four centuries, acting as a boundary between the parishes of St Paul and St Pancras (Plate 4).

The seventeenth century
Archaeologically this century is marked by the ubiquitous appearance of the clay pipe, of which a large number of examples have been found. In the Pancras Lane garden area a new set of rubble-filled trenches was dug, and these run up to what seems to be a garden shed built up against the boundary wall. Part of the area to the east of the wall was also apparently garden, with a large open drain next to the wall. In one part of the garden there were several cess-pits, some as late as the eighteenth century, but now internal latrines were regular, constructed of blocks of Heavitree stone. One, infilled with clay, contained a silver spoon with trefoil handle (Plate 8). It was stamped with four Exeter town marks, and later had the initials K.B. and the date 1680 punched on the handle. The junction of stem and bowl is decorated with an elaborate acanthus, the spoon being one of only two of this type known with Exeter marks.

The open drain against the boundary wall was eventually filled in and a narrow building constructed against the wall. The new footings include moulded stones, perhaps from a church, and it is worth noting that St Paul's, just up the road, was reconstructed about this time. This narrow building was used for some industrial purpose, as over the floor lay a great mass of broken crockery, resembling flower pot in texture, from two types of vessel: large cauldrons with tripod feet, and smaller conical vessels with pointed bases, which are most likely to be moulds for making sugar loaves. The building was destroyed about 1700.

The eighteenth century

In terms of structures, this century is less well represented than even the earlier phases. On the Goldsmith Street frontage only a single small cellar dating from the end of the century was excavated (GS 47–44), and there are also a few cess pits. Amongst the pottery, the slipped vessels of South Somerset (e.g. Donyatt) are well represented, and there are occasional 'Westerwald' stonewares from the Rhine. In the Pancras Lane garden yet a third series of trenches were cut. A new building was constructed against the boundary wall with walls of stone and brick, a slate roof with pottery ridge tiles, and glazed windows.

Roads and terracing

Frequent mention has been made of how much of the deposits has been lost in terracing. Often the modern rubble directly overlies Roman deposits, a phenomenon of regular occurrence in Exeter, in contrast to ancient towns elsewhere, such as Winchester and London where archaeological deposits are often of considerable depth. The reason seems to be a combination of the impervious subsoil, and a failure to maintain street surfaces in post-medieval times, to which several visitors such as Defoe allude. The result has been that several streets have become hollow-ways cutting down into the underlying deposits. The extreme example is Paul Street, which seems to have dropped some 2–3 metres. House platforms have then been terraced back into the sides of these hollow ways, leading to a general drop in ground level. The problem seems to have developed in the seventeenth century, as the earlier garden deposits follow the level natural contours and are actually cut by Pancras Lane. The terrace walls are largely of early-nineteenth century date, so erosion must have taken place fairly rapidly.

Conclusions

A military origin for the lay-out of Roman Exeter now seems a distinct possibility. The pattern of the later civil property boundaries appears to be based on the military layout, with the building lines following those of the supposed barrack blocks. By the beginning of the second century the town was expanding rapidly, with sophisticated timber buildings, later to be replaced by stone. In common with other Roman towns there is evidence for a radical economic change in the fourth century, with the disappearance of many of the town houses, and the appearance of agriculture or animal husbandry within the city walls. The precise date and function of the linear gullies escapes us; they could be late Roman or Saxon. After the late fourth century, the next unambiguous evidence of habitation belongs to the eleventh century and by the twelfth century the present road system, independent of the Roman streets, has already been laid out. Expansion in this period was rapid, and within a hundred years the majority of Goldsmith Street was built up and trade was beginning to flourish.

The 1972 excavations are certain to add appreciably to the picture, if not fundamentally to alter it. If we can obtain more of the plan of the early timber buildings we may be able to place their military origin beyond all doubt. We may be able to obtain a relatively complete plan of some of the civil buildings, but especially we must hope for evidence for the period between the fourth and twelfth centuries. We shall also have good samples of the medieval occupation over the whole area, and understand better the process of colonization and also the relative social status of the various areas.

Acknowledgements
The excavations were jointly conducted by Exeter University and Exeter City Council, with additional financial assistance from the Department of the Environment. Supervision of the finances was undertaken by Professor Barlow, head of the Department of History, and Mr Patrick Boylan, Director of the City Museum. Lady (Aileen) Fox and my co-director Mr Michael Griffiths have been continuous sources of help and advice, and the latter took over responsibility for the final stages of the excavation. To all these I wish to express my thanks as well as to the many officers and staff of the City Council and University who freely gave specialist assistance. I must also mention the many volunteers whose hard work produced the results, the site supervisors and assistants, Misses Ann Gentry, Sarah Holgate and Linda Hollingworth, Mrs Sissel Collis and Messrs. Graham Black, Stuart May, John Reading, Tim Shepherd, Eric Wayman, David Whipp, and especially Chris Henderson who ran the excavation during the difficult winter months; and the photographer, Mr Robert Turner formerly of the Department of History. Finally I wish to thank Dr Joyce Youings and Miss Ann Hamlin who have devoted much time and trouble to preparing the manuscript for publication.

ISBN 978-1-80413-184-8 Paperback
ISBN 978-1-80413-185-5 PDF

www.ingramcontent.com/pod-product-compliance
Lightning Source LLC
Chambersburg PA
CBHW031448280326
41927CB00037B/401